D0585531

BASKETBALL

PLAY·THE·GAME

BASKETBALL

David Titmuss •

WARD LOCK

First published in Great Britain in 1989
by Ward Lock Limited, 8 Clifford Street,
London W1X 1RB, a Cassell Company

Reprinted 1990

Series editor Ian Morrison
Designed by Anita Ruddell
Illustrations by Bob Williams

Text set in Helvetica
by Hourds Typographica, Stafford, England
Printed in England by Clays Ltd, St Ives plc

British Library Cataloguing in Publication Data
Titmuss, David
   Basketball. – (Play the game).
   1. Basketball, – Manuals
   I. Title   II. Series
   796. 32'32

ISBN 0-7063-6768-5

Acknowledgments

The publishers would like to thank
Colorsport for providing all the pictures
except those on pages 65 and 73 which were
provided by Sporting Pictures (UK) Ltd.

Frontispiece: **Vern Fleming, a guard with
the US Olympic team of 1984 making a
stunning fast break.**

CONTENTS

FOREWORD

On behalf of the English Basket Ball Association I am delighted to endorse and highly recommend this excellent book to all aspiring basketballers. The crisp text and clear illustrations ensure that its meaning is readily accessible to the novice and an ideal refresher for the more experienced performer.

The history of the sport is well documented and makes fascinating reading. Basketball equipment is thoroughly covered so that, when you first walk on to a court, you will be familiar with the surroundings. There are some peculiar terms unique to basketball, and these are covered in an interesting terminology section. The rules of basketball are covered in a simple Game Guide but for those of you who want to delve into the finer points and intricacies which all rules have, then no stone is unturned in the cleverly designed Rules Clinic. The remainder of the book is devoted to basketball technique.

I can think of no one more suitable to write about the sport of basketball than the author, David Titmuss, who is one of the country's most knowledgeable, talented and committed coaches. His work with the English Senior Men's team, which under his leadership enjoyed a period of unprecedented success, firmly established his international reputation. Coach Titmuss holds the English Basket Ball Association's Senior Coach award, is a frequent lecturer at advanced coach training courses and has considerable practical experience coaching in the USA, with the England team, and in Europe on both sides of the iron curtain. He has recently returned to working in Britain's professional basketball league where, in 1986, he was voted Coach of the Year and currently manages and coaches the Hemel Hempstead and Watford Royals Club in Hertfordshire.

Brian E. Coleman
Senior Technical Officer,
English Basket Ball Association

HISTORY &
DEVELOPMENT OF
BASKETBALL

Unlike many sports, basketball can pinpoint its exact origins to one day in 1891 when Canadian-born Dr James Naismith invented a brand new game, as opposed to evolving it from another sport.

Naismith was a leader of the International YMCA Training School at Springfield, Massachussetts and was set the task of devising a new game for his students who were fed up with conventional forms of gymnastics. And so he set about inventing his new game which, because the basic principal was to secure possession of the ball and throw it into the opponents' basket, he called basketball.

Although Naismith's game was brand new, evidence suggests that he got his idea from other, older sports.

A form of basketball was played in ancient Central and South American civilizations. Playing courts bounded by stone walls and set among trees have been found on the Yucatan peninsular of South America dating to the seventh century BC. The game, known as *pok-tapok*, took place as part of a religious festival. It was played with a ball filled with sacred plants and the ball had to be hit into an elevated 'goal' using only the knees, thighs, and hips. The goals consisted of a flat slab with a hole in the middle and it was through this hole that the ball had to pass . . . a bit like scoring a basket in basketball.

In Mexico, in the sixteenth century, the game of *Ollamalitzli* was similar, but played with a solid rubber ball being thrown through a stone ring. Rumour has it that the player who successfully threw the ball into the ring could claim the clothes of all spectators . . . a bit like strip basketball!

A seventeenth-century engraving depicts a game similar to basketball and the *Encylopedia of Athletics* (1818) lists a game played in Florida in which players threw a ball into a basket attached to the top of a pole.

Despite these precedents, though, there is no denying that credit for the playing of basketball as we know it today goes to Dr Naismith.

Naismith wanted a game which prevented physical contact and consequently running with the ball was outlawed in his first set of rules. Naismith also saw his game demanding skill and not physical strength. That is still the case today, although it does help to be strong and above average height.

Simplicity was uppermost in Naismith's mind when he drew up his first set of rules in December 1891. A look at his first rules will bear this out. But closer examination of his rules, and cross reference with the Game Guide on pages 25–36 will show that many of his original 13 rules form the basis of the present-day game.

BASKETBALL'S · FIRST · RULES

1 The ball, an ordinary Association football, may be thrown in any direction with one or both hands.

2 The ball may be batted in any direction with one or both hands, but never with the fist.

3 A player cannot run with the ball. The player must throw it from the spot on which he catches it. Allowance to be made for the man who catches the ball while running at a good speed.

4 The ball must be held in or between the hands. The arms or the body must not be used for holding it.

5 No shouldering, holding, pushing, striking or tripping in any way the person of an opponent shall be allowed. The first infringement of this rule by any person shall count as a foul; the second shall disqualify him until the next goal is made or, if there was evident intent to injure the person, for the whole of the game. No substitution shall be allowed.

6 A foul is striking at the ball with the fist, violations of rules 3 and 4, and such as described in rule 5.

7 If either side makes three consecutive fouls it shall count as a goal for the opponents (consecutive means without the opponents in the meantime making a foul).

8 A goal shall be made when the ball is thrown or batted from the ground into the basket and stays there, providing those defending the goal do not touch or disturb the goal. If the ball rests on the edge and the opponents move the basket it shall count as a goal.

9 When the ball goes out of bounds it shall be thrown into the field and played by the first person touching it. In case of dispute the umpire shall throw it straight into the field, the thrower-in is allowed five seconds. If he holds it longer it shall go to the opponents. If any side persists in delaying the game, the umpire shall call a foul on them.

Meadowlark Lemon, one of the all-time greats from the Harlem Globetrotters delighting the crowd.

10 The umpire shall be the judge of the men and shall note the fouls and notify the referee when three consecutive fouls have been made. He shall have the power to disqualify men according to rule 5.

11 The referee shall be the judge of the ball and decide when it is in play in bounds, to which side it belongs, and shall keep the time. He shall decide when a goal has been made and keep account of the goals with any other duties that are usually performed by a referee.

12 The time shall be two 15 minute halves with five minutes rest between.

13 The side making the most goals in that time shall be declared the winners.

It was to these rules of 20 January 1892 that the first game of basketball took place at the Springfield YMCA gymnasium. Two peach baskets nailed to a balcony 10ft (3m) from the ground were installed and these formed the goals. Being out of reach from the players it was another example of the new game demanding the best of skills from the player who was required to throw the ball accurately into the 'goal'.

Surprisingly Naismith's rules did not stipulate how many players were on a side. He suggested any number between three and forty could play. But that first game at Springfield consisted of nine students per team and this was felt to be an ideal number at first.

Basketball proved to be so popular that other colleges and organizations requested copies of Naismith's rules.

Basketball had arrived and its early success lay in its simplicity and the fact that it could be played on any area, large or small. The year after its debut at Springfield the first game of basketball was played in England when it was introduced by Mme Bergman-Osterberg at Hampstead Physical Training College.

By 1895 players had become so skilled it was agreed that the number in a team should be restricted to either five, seven, or nine, depending upon the size of the playing area available. But it was not long before this was standardized at today's figure of five.

Also, in 1895, the YMCA obtained a copy of the rules and modified them slightly for their women members to provide a less strenuous game, thus bringing about the birth of netball.

Naismith had developed one of the most popular participant sports but he overlooked one important detail: how to retrieve the ball every time a 'goal' was scored. Initially a ladder was used to get the ball out of the basket. But, as players got better, and goals were scored more frequently, a lot of time was wasted with retrieving the ball. Towards the end of the century, however, the basket was replaced by a metal ring which had a bottomless net attached to it. And so the basketball ball retriever was made redundant. Oh well, that's life!

Right from the start, basketball competitions were organized through the YMCA movement, and in 1901 the first collegiate league was inaugurated. Basketball made its debut as a demonstration sport at the 1904 St Louis Olympics but all teams were from the United States. However, when it was included as an exhibition sport at the Paris Olympics of 1924, teams from France, Italy, United States and Great Britain competed. The London Central YMCA won the gold medal. Despite efforts, largely those of Dr Forest Allen, to get basketball included at the 1928, and then 1932, Olympics as either a full or demonstration sport, it was neglected on both occasions.

However, the sport gained credibility in 1932 when the international ruling body, the International Amateur Basketball Federation (Federation Internationale de Basketball Amateur – FIBA) was formed. Seven countries attended a meeting at Geneva and Renato William Jones (Italian-born son of an Englishman) was appointed the first secretary-general. Today there are more

than 178 member nations of FIBA.

Allen and Jones were successful in their attempts to get basketball included in the XIth Olympics at Berlin in 1936. Twenty-two nations competed in the first full Olympic tournament which, unusually, was played outdoors. The United States were the first champions and one of the referees was Avery Brundage, later to become the President of the International Olympic Committee. The medals were presented by the game's inventor, Dr Naismith, who died three years later at the age of 78.

The game soon spread worldwide after gaining Olympic status, thanks largely to the efforts of the YMCA movement and American servicemen who introduced the sport at each of their 'ports-of-call'.

Minor adjustments were made to Naismith's rules over the years. Dribbling became legal; a backboard was added behind the basket, thus making rebounding an important part of the game, and the ball became unique in size and weight, as opposed to using a standard association football.

Two other significant rule changes were introduced. The first in the 1920s saw the introduction of the rule that the player fouled had to take free shots himself. Previously, a specialist 'free-shooter' was employed. And in 1936 the jump-ball, which was used at the centre circle after every score was abolished. Consequently, the game was speeded up and became more strenuous.

Specific timing regulations, time-outs, and increase in size of the restricted area under the basket have all been important changes and additions which have helped to make basketball one of the best spectator sports.

In America, spectators have ample opportunity to watch basketball at the highest level. The NCAA (Collegiate game) has organized its championship since 1938 and the National Basketball Association (NBA) gained Major League status in 1949, although the professional game was born in the United States at the turn of the twentieth

century. The NBA offers all that is best in the professional game while the entertaining Harlem Globetrotters team provide circus-like performances.

Known the world over as 'the trotters', they were formed by Abraham Saperstein in 1927 who took his team of all-black players around the United States giving exhibitions and demonstrations. They gradually introduced skilful and entertaining routines into their play, which eventually developed into a comedy routine with such well-known exponents as Meadowlark Lemon. They adopted the music of 'Sweet Georgia Brown' as their theme tune, and it has been heard in most countries world-wide as the Globetrotters have taken their own special brand of entertainment to all corners of the globe.

In Great Britain the English Basket Ball Association was founded in 1936 and Holylake YMCA were the first winners of the National Championship. The YMCA movement has played a crucial role in basketball's development in Britain as well as in the United States. The Scottish, Irish and Welsh associations were formed as independent Associations in 1947, 1946 and 1956 respectively.

The sport dropped in popularity in Britain in the early 1960s. But a dramatic growth period got under way in the 1970s when the English Basket Ball Association appointed its first full-time administrator, Mel Welch.

Club sponsorship came into the British game in a big way in 1973, and in 1975 attendances broke the 100,000 barrier. Famous names have been brought into basketball, and the Manchester United, Bolton Wanderers and Glasgow Rangers football teams have acquired franchises over the years. The end-of-season play-offs are the highlight of the season in Britain and, until 1989 when the 'Final Four' tournament moved to the NEC at Birmingham, were played at Wembley Arena.

Women also play basketball – and not only netball, as many people believe. The women's game was included in the Olympic programme for the first time in 1976. They have also had their own World Championships since 1953, coming just three years after Argentina won the inaugural men's World Championship.

Basketball is growing in popularity all the time, both as a participant and spectator sport. As a participant sport there is no restriction put on the aspirant player. Certainly, most basketball players are tall, but don't let that put you off because there is always a place for the skilful player, irrespective of size. As a spectator sport, basketball offers all the excitement that other team sports like soccer can provide but with three additional important factors. First, being played on a smaller area, all the action can be seen at close range . . . and indoors. Second, there is always a result, there are no draws in basketball. Third, basketball matches are places of family entertainment. Men, women and children can attend a basketball match and mix with supporters of opposing sides and the air of friendliness is maintained. A sport offering that these days can only be a good one to get involved with.

Play the Game: Basketball will give you an insight into the game whether it be as an aspiring youngster wishing to take the game up, or as the spectator who wants to enjoy the thrills and excitement of basketball from a cosy position either in the stands or in your armchair. Either way, *Play the Game* will improve your knowledge of the game.

EQUIPMENT & TERMINOLOGY

Before we introduce you to the rules of basketball, you ought to familiarize yourself with the playing area, playing equipment and some of the terminology you will encounter when playing or watching the game. Let's start with the court.

The court

Basketball can be played indoors or outdoors. But at senior and international level it is exclusively an indoor game.

The playing area, known as the court, is rectangular and should be a level, hard surface and free from any obstructions which may be dangerous to the players. Ideally the playing surface should be wood or any suitable artificial surface that will provide the ball with a good and consistent bounce.

The court measures 26m (85ft) in length and 14m (46ft) in width. Variations of plus or minus 2m (6ft 6in) on length and 1m (3ft) on width are permitted but any variations must be proportional to each other. You can't add 2m (6ft 6in) to the length but reduce the width by 1m (3ft).

A clearance of 7m (24ft) between the floor and ceiling should exist and the court

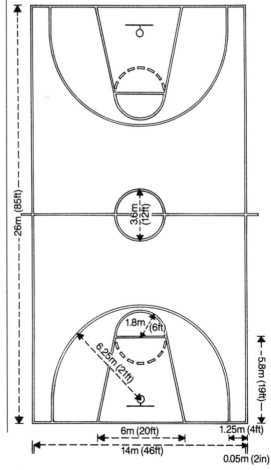

The court

26m (85ft)

3.6m (12ft)

1.8m (6ft)

6.25m (21ft)

5.8m (19ft)

6m (20ft)

1.25m (4ft)

14m (46ft)

0.05m (2in)

BASKETBALL

The free-throw area

All lines 0.05m (2in) wide

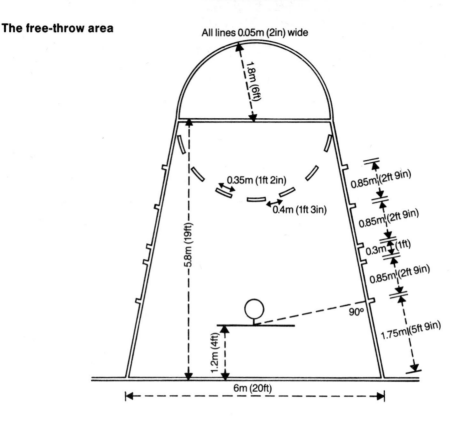

1.8m (6ft)

0.35m (1ft 2in)

0.4m (1ft 3in)

5.8m (19ft)

0.85m (2ft 9in)

0.85m (2ft 9in)

0.3m (1ft)

0.85m (2ft 9in)

90°

1.75m (5ft 9in)

1.2m (4ft)

6m (20ft)

should be adequately lit and no unsightly shadows cast. The lighting should not be so positioned that it will hinder the vision and sight of any of the players or officials.

The court should be bounded by boundary lines at least 2m (6ft 6in) from any obstructions including seating, scorers'/timekeepers' tables, etc. The lines that extend along the length of the court are known as the **side lines** and those across the width are the **end lines**. All boundary lines should be clearly marked and be 5cm (2in) wide.

One of the three *restraining circles*, with a radius of 1.8m (6ft), is drawn at the centre of the court. The court is divided into two equal halves by a centre-line which extends beyond the side-lines by 15cm (6in). The centre-line provides each team with a *front court* and a *back court*. A team's front court

is that part of the court between the opponents' end-line and the nearer edge of the centre-line. Their back court is the other half of the court *including* the centre-line. The front and back courts are important as you will find out later when we discuss the rules in detail in the Game Guide on pages 25–36.

The *free-throw line* is basketball's equivalent to the penalty spot in soccer. It is a line 3.6m (12ft) long drawn parallel to the end-line and is 5.8m (19ft) from the inner edge of the end-line to the further edge of the free-throw line. The centre of the free-throw line should be in line with the centre point of the end-line.

At each end of the court is a *restricted area*; again its importance will become clear in the Game Guide section. The area is bounded by lines drawn from each end of the free-throw line to a point 3m (10ft) either side of the centre of the end-line. The restricted area is further extended by a semi-circle drawn from the centre of the free-throw line and with a radius of 1.8m (6ft). The semi-circle extends into the restricted area to make a complete circle, but that part of the circle in the restricted area is shown only by a broken line. These two circles form the other restraining circles.

During free throws players must stand at spaces marked along the restricted area. The first of these spaces is marked 1.8m (6ft) from the inside edge of the end-line. The others are as per the diagram opposite.

Because basketball now has a three-point basket (see Terminology) the area from where such a score can be made is defined by the drawing of an arc with a radius of 6.25m (20ft 4in) from the centre of the basket. It forms a semi-circle with each end terminating at the end-line.

The basket and backboard

The *backboard* is 1.2m (4ft) from the end-line and measures 1.8m × 1.2m (6ft × 4ft). It should be made of hard wood 3cm (1in) thick or of a suitable transparent material but with a similar rigidity to wood. The front surface must be flat and white (unless it is transparent). A rectangle measuring 59cm × 45cm (2ft × 1ft 6in) should be drawn on the backboard. The bottom line of the rectangle should be level with the top of the net. The lines of this rectangle should be 5cm (2in) wide. A 5cm (2in) border should be drawn along the outside perimeter of the backboard and in a colour contrasting with the background.

The backboard should be positioned above the court and with its lower edge 2.75m (9ft) above the floor. The backboard should be positioned at a central point between the two side-lines and the supports should be at least 1m (3ft) outside the end-line painted in a colour contrasting with the background so players can easily see

The ball

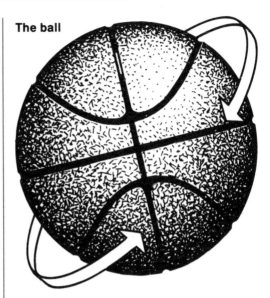

Circumference: 75–78cm (29½–30¼in)
Weight: 600–650gm (20–22oz)

the backboard. In the interest of safety it should also be covered in a padded protective material.

Attached to each backboard is the all-important *basket*. The ring which supports the net (or basket) is made of solid iron, has an inside diameter of 45cm (1ft 6in) and should be painted orange. The ring should be rigidly attached to the backboard and at a point 3.05m (10ft) above the floor. The net, which is attached to the ring, is made of cord and is 40cm (15in) long. It should be wide enough for the ball to freely pass through.

The ball

The ball is round and the outer casing should be either leather, rubber or other suitable synthetic material. Its circumference should be between 75 and 78cm (29½ and 30¼in) and its weight between 600 and 650gm (20 and 22oz). It should be inflated to a pressure so that when it is dropped from a height of 1.8m (6ft) (measured from the floor to the bottom of the ball) on to the playing

BASKETBALL

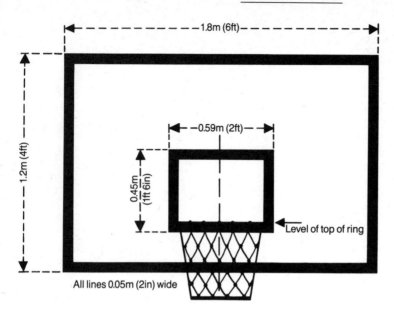

1.8m (6ft)

1.2m (4ft)

0.59m (2ft)

0.45m (1ft 6in)

Level of top of ring

All lines 0.05m (2in) wide

surface, it will rebound to a height of between 1.2 and 1.4m (4ft and 4ft 7in), (measured to the top of the ball).

In addition to that equipment already mentioned, the home team is normally responsible for providing the following: a clock, time-out watch, device for displaying to players and spectators how much time is left on the 30-seconds rule (see Game Guide), an official score sheet, scoreboard

The backboard and basket

Note the rectangular 'marker' directly above the basket.

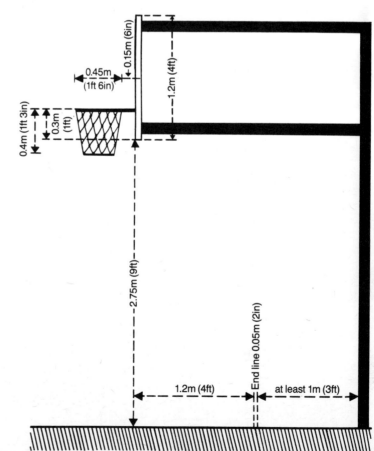

0.45m (1ft 6in)

0.15m (6in)

1.2m (4ft)

0.4m (1ft 3in)

0.3m (1ft)

2.75m (9ft)

1.2m (4ft)

End line 0.05m (2in)

at least 1m (3ft)

The basket and support.

visible to spectators and players, markers displaying the numbers 1 to 5 for use by the scorer to indicate how many fouls a player commits, and two team-foul markers which are red and placed on the scorer's table to indicate a seventh-player foul by a team.

Clothing

Players of each team should wear the same outfits which must not clash with the opposing team. Each player should wear a numbered shirt and no two players in the same team should wear the same number. Players are numbered between 4 and 15. Loose-fitting shorts for mobility, and sleeveless vests are the standard attire. Basketball shoes should be rubber-soled and with protected ankle supports, although these are not necessary. Most important of all, make sure your clothing is comfortable. It is important to wear towelled socks; and it is not a bad idea to buy a pair of shoes a little too big to enable you to wear two pairs of socks which will reduce the risk of blistering.

Right, that's basketball equipment. Now for some terms you will encounter:

Shoes

Note the rubber soles for good traction.

Clothing

TERMINOLOGY

Assist   A pass which allows the receiver an easy, close score.

Back court   The half of the court containing a team's basket.

Back court violation   When the team in possession passes the ball back into their own half of the court.

Baseball pass   A single-handed, overhead pass in which the ball is thrown in a motion similar to the throw of a baseball.

Basket   The basket is basketball's goal. It is also the term used to denote a successful score. A successful basket is worth either one, two or three points.

Centre   Sometimes the key player in a team. He is usually, but not always, the tallest player and should be capable of scoring from close range and from rebounds. He is also known as the pivot.

Charged time-out   Coaches may request two *time-outs* per half, each one lasting up to one minute during which time they can instruct their players. If a game goes into

The baseball pass

Use it to throw long distances.

Stephen Bontraeger who pioneered the way for the three-point rule when it was first introduced to England.

overtime, then one time-out is allowed per extra period played.

Disqualifying foul   Any blatant disregard for the rules and unsportsmanlike conduct will result in a player being removed from the game permanently.

Double foul   When two players from opposing sides commit personal fouls against each other. Play is re-started with a *jump-ball*.

Double team   Term used when two defenders mark one attacker.

Dunk   When a basket is scored by a player jumping with the ball above the net and thrusting it down through the net. Also known as a *'stuff'*.

Fake   A dummy with the body and/or ball in order to wrong-foot your opponent.

Fast break   A quick move out of defence after gaining possession of the ball and designed to take the opposing team by surprise before they have a chance to re-form their defence.

Field goal   A scoring shot from open play. It is worth either two or three points.

Five-second rule   A closely guarded player in possession of the ball must pass, shoot or dribble the ball within five seconds of gaining possession.

Forwards   Tall players who take up a position in the *front court*, normally between the side-lines and restricted area.

Free throw   A free throw at the *basket* without any interference from the opposing team. The throw is taken from the free-throw line and each successful throw is worth one point. Free throws are awarded for rule infringements.

The free throw

Front court   The half of the court in which your opponent's basket is situated, and the half of the court your team attacks.

Full court press   A defensive tactic employing the entire court not just the *back court*.

Guards   Usually smaller than the forwards, the guards are good dribblers and passers. They should be excellent ball-handlers, and also be able to shoot accurately from long distance. The guard is the playmaker of the side.

Held ball   When two or more players of opposing teams have one or both hands firmly on the ball at the same time.

Intentional foul   A personal foul which, in the opinion of the official, was deliberate. In addition to the offending player having a personal foul charged against him, two *free throws* are awarded.

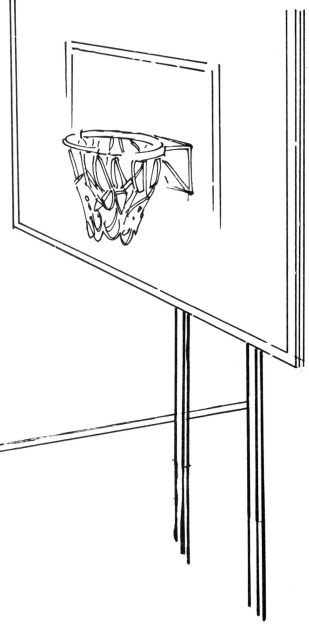

BASKETBALL

Jump ball   A method of starting, and re-starting play. The ball is thrown up by an official between two opposing players who have to attempt to gain possession for their team.

Key   The restricted area. It is called the key because it resembles a keyhole. The semi-circle forms part of the key.

Man-to-man marking   A form of defence whereby a defensive player marks a specific attacking player rather than defending an opponent only when he moves into a particular area of court.

Multiple foul   When two or more team-mates commit a personal foul against the same opponent . . . a bit unfair, I know, but it does happen!

Outlet pass   The first pass of the defensive team after a rebound. Often it is a quick pass out to a player near to the side line.

Out-of-bounds   A player or the ball is out-of-bounds if he/it touches the floor on or outside the boundary lines.

Out-of-bounds

A player is deemed to be out-of-bounds if part of his foot is on, or over, a side- or end-line.

Overtime   Drawn games do not exist in basketball. So, if the scores are level at the end of normal time extra periods of overtime, each lasting five minutes, are played.

Personal foul   A foul against an opponent whether the ball is in play, alive or dead. Blocking, holding, pushing, charging, tripping, and impeding, all constitute personal fouls.

Pivot   See *centre*.

Strong side   The side of the court in which the attacking team has possession of the ball.

Stuff   See *dunk*.

Substitutes   Up to five substitutes per team are allowed.

A personal foul

Deliberately trying to hinder your opponent is a personal foul.

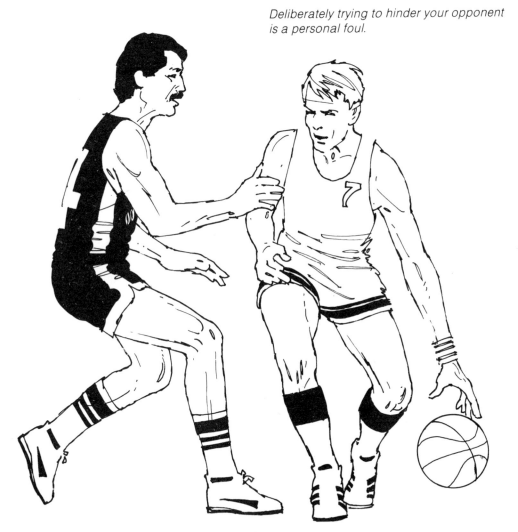

Technical foul   Can be committed by either a player, coach, substitutes or team followers. Anything which is against the spirit of the game can be basically described as a technical foul.

Ten-seconds rule   Within ten seconds of getting the ball a team must advance the ball over the half-way line.

Three-point basket   A basket scored from open play outside the three-point arc.

Three-point play   When a player is fouled in the process of scoring a two-point basket and gains another point from the *free throw*.

Three-seconds rule   No player may stand in that part of the opposing restricted area between the end-line and free-throw line for more than three seconds when his own team has possession of the ball.

Time-out   A time-out can be called by a coach when the clock is stopped after an official signals: (a) a violation, (b) a foul, (c) a *held ball*, (d) unusual delay in re-starting game following a deadball, (e) suspension of play following injury, (f) suspension of play for any other reason, (g) when the thirty-seconds signal is sounded, (h) after a basket is scored against the team which has requested a *charged time-out*.

Weak side   The side of the court opposite where the attacking side has possession of the ball.

Zone defence   The marking of attacking players when they move into specific areas of the court as opposed to man-to-man marking.

THE GAME – A GUIDE

Basketball is a fast moving, all-action game. The object is simple; to get the ball into the opposing net in order to score points. But to get into a scoring position the ball must be dribbled or passed around the court using the hands only. That is when it starts getting a bit more difficult.

As we have already seen, a team consists of no more than ten players, with five only on court at any one time. However, in tournaments where a team has to play more than five games, then the number of players in each team may be increased to twelve.

One member of the team is appointed the captain. If, for any reason, the captain leaves the court then he must inform the referee which team-mate will take over his role.

Officials

A game of basketball is controlled by a referee and umpire who are assisted by a timekeeper, scorer and a thirty-second operator. The officials should wear basketball shoes, long grey trousers and a grey shirt so as to be easily distinguishable from the players.

The **referee and umpire** jointly control the game and take up positions on opposite sides of the court so they can see all of the action (and infringements) between them. Before each jump-ball and after each foul they swap sides. The referee has ultimate control and he is the official who makes a decision on any point not specifically mentioned in the rules of the game.

The **scorer** also plays an important role. In addition to keeping a chronological check of points scored he must also record the personal and technical fouls called against each player. He also keeps a note of the time-outs charged to each team, notes the starting line-ups of each team and any subsequent changes in playing personnel by way of substitutions. He's certainly a busy lad is the scorer!

The **timekeeper** keeps a record of playing time and time of stoppage(s) as provided within the rules. He is also responsible for timing the time-outs and for indicating the end of each half or overtime.

The final official is the **thirty-seconds operator**. He operates the thirty-second clock which is started by him the moment a team takes possession of the ball.

Right. They are the officials. Let's now see how the game is played.

BASKETBALL

Officials' signals

Two points.	Three points attempt.	Three points – successful shot.	Cancel score/Cancel play.
Time out.	Charged time-out.	Substitution.	Time in.
Travelling.	Illegal dribble.	Three-seconds rule – infraction.	Personal foul.
Personal foul. No free throws.	Free throw penalty.	To designate offender.	Pushing.

Illegal use of hands.

Holding.

Blocking.

Charging.

Foul by team in control of the ball.

Technical foul.

Intentional foul.

Disqualifying foul.

Double foul.

Jump ball.

Ball returned to back court.

Three free throws.

Two free throws.

One free throw.

One-and-one penalty.

Resetting of thirty-seconds clock.

BASKETBALL

The game is divided into two halves, each lasting 20 minutes and with an interval of (normally) 10 minutes.

The game is started with a jump-ball in the centre circle. The visiting team has choice of baskets in the first half. Ends are changed after the interval. If the game is played at a neutral venue then a choice of baskets in the first half is decided by the toss of a coin.

The jump-ball starts each subsequent half or extra period of play. It is performed by the referee throwing the ball up into the air between two opposing players who each stand in that half of the centre circle nearer to their own basket.

The ball cannot be touched until it has reached its greatest height. A player involved in the jump-ball may touch the ball twice only. He must not touch it again until one of the eight players not included in the jump-ball has touched it, or it has touched the floor, ring or backboard. All non-jumpers must stand outside the centre circle.

Once a team has possession of the ball,

The jump-ball

The jump-ball is used to start the game.

Paul Stimpson, England's most capped player, demonstrating use of his weak hand.

the player with the ball may dribble it by bouncing it on the ground using one hand to do so. He may, alternatively, pass it to a team-mate. The eventual aim is to get the ball to a player in a suitable position to shoot at the net in the hope of successfully scoring points.

If the ball is successfully thrown through the net it is worth three points if thrown from outside the three-point line, otherwise it is worth two points. A goal from a free throw (which will be explained later) is worth one point. The winning team is the team scoring the most points, NOT the team obtaining the most baskets.

After a field goal has been scored, play is not re-started with another jump-ball. The ball is returned to play by a member of the non-scoring team who stands at a point out-of-bounds at the end of the court where the goal was made. Play is also re-started by this method after the last free throw, if successful. If the ball goes out of play over the side lines it is returned by a member of the team who did not last play the ball by means of a throw-in.

Play resumes until the end of 40 minutes playing time and the team with the most points is deemed the winner. However, if the scores are level at the end of normal playing time then an extra period of five minutes is played. As many extra periods as required to find a winner are played. There is no limit on the number of extra periods.

Timing regulations

To ensure basketball maintains its fluency and that the 40 minutes is actually utilized as playing time, there are various timing regulations which are observed.

To indicate the start of a game the clock is activated the moment the ball reaches its highest point at the jump-ball. The game clock is stopped at the end of each half or extra period when the official blows his whistle for any of the following:

(a) a violation

(b) a foul
(c) a held ball
(d) delay in re-starting game following a dead-ball
(e) suspension of play following injury
(f) suspension of play for any reason as ordered by the officials
(g) when the thirty-second signal is sounded
(h) when a field goal is scored against the team whose coach has requested a time-out

Charged time-outs are permitted by a team's coach. He is allowed to call a maximum of two per half and must indicate his request to the scorer who conveys the request to the officials. As soon as the ball becomes dead the clock is stopped and the charged time-out lasting one minute begins. It is important to realise, for timing purposes, when a ball is in play and when it is alive.

The ball is in play when: (a) the official enters the centre circle to carry out the jump-ball; (b) the official enters the free throw area to effect a free throw, or (c) the player at a throw-in has taken up an out-of-bounds position and taken possession of the ball.

In the above instances the ball becomes alive when: (a) the ball, having reached its highest peak at the jump-ball, is touched by a player involved in the jump-ball, (b) the official gives the ball to a player entitled to take the free throw, or (c) the ball touches a player in play from a throw-in.

The following timings are important and should be fully understood:

The three-seconds rule   A player must not remain for more than three seconds in that part of the opponent's restricted area between the end-line and furthest edge of the free-throw line, while his team is in control of the ball.

The five-seconds rule   A closely guarded player who does not pass, shoot, roll or dribble the ball within five seconds shall be penalized and have a violation called

The dribble

Dribbling is one way of moving the ball around the court – but passing is better.

against him. A player out-of-bounds must put the ball in play within five seconds or possession goes to the defensive team.

The ten-seconds rule   When a team gains possession of a live ball in its own back court it must, within ten seconds, cause the ball to go into its front court. If it does not then a violation is called. If a team has possession in its front court, it must not cause the ball to go into its own back court.

The thirty-seconds rule   Within thirty seconds of gaining control of a live ball a team must shoot at goal. Failure to do so is violation.

Any violations are penalized with loss of ball to the opposing team.

Pivotting

When making a forward pivot, left foot 'A' moves to position 'A1' and right foot 'B' stays in position but pivots through 180°.

The same happens in the reverse pivot except the right foot pivots in the opposite direction.

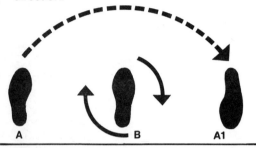

Moving the ball around the court

First, it must be remembered that the ball can only be played with the hands. Touching the ball with the leg or foot is a violation, unless it is accidental. The ball must not be played with a clenched fist, nor must it be carried.

When dribbling, the ball must be bounced onto the floor and with one hand only. The dribble is deemed to have ended when a player touches the ball with both hands simultaneously, or allows the ball to come to rest in one or both hands. He may not dribble again until after he has taken a shot or the ball has been played by another person.

When a player gets possession of the ball from another player, or from a rebounded attempt at a basket, he will be either standing still or on the move.

If he is standing still when he receives the ball he can either dribble the ball, pass it, or shoot. If he chooses either of the latter two options then he cannot move with the ball. However, he can pivot. This means one foot must remain in position on the ground while the other is moved, which results in the body pivoting.

If the ball is collected while on the move the player cannot progress more than two steps without bouncing or dribbling the ball.

It is important to come to a legal stop when collecting the ball on the move or at the end of a dribble and the **two-count rhythm** is employed.

The first count occurs: (a) as a player receives the ball, if either foot is touching the floor at the same time that he receives it, or (b) as either foot touches the floor, or as both feet touch the floor, if both feet are off the floor when he receives it.

The second count occurs when, after the first count, either foot touches the floor or both feet touch the floor simultaneously. However, if a player comes to a stop after the first count, he is not entitled to the second count.

When a player comes to a legal stop he may then pivot, but using the back foot *only* as a pivot. If neither foot is ahead of the other, he can use either foot as the pivot.

The two-count rhythm

Once a foot has touched the floor that is 'Count 1'. The second count is when the other foot touches the floor. You must then stop. If you pivot it will be on the right foot (the back one).

Basketball is theoretically a no-contact sport. But contact between players, either deliberately or accidentally, does occur and the rules make provisions for such incidents.

A **personal foul** is called against a player who makes contact with an opponent at any time whether the ball is alive or dead. A personal foul constitutes blocking, tripping, pushing, charging, or holding up the progress of an opponent by extending an arm, shoulder, hip or knee, or by bending the body into an other than normal position. Rough tactics should certainly never be used.

A foul will be called if contact with the hands is made with an opponent. However, if contact is only with the opponent's hand which is touching the ball, then no foul will be called provided the contact was made while attempting to get the ball.

If a player has five fouls called against him in a game, whether they be personal or technical fouls, he must leave the game. After seven player fouls (either personal or technical) have been called against a team in one half, then the **one-and-one rule** is brought into force. This means that when a player commits a foul after the introduction of the rule, the player fouled has the right to two free throws, but he must score the first attempt in order to get a second.

The free throw

A free throw is called against a team who commits a foul. The free throw is taken from a point behind the free-throw line and in the case of a personal foul being called then the player fouled must take the throw. If a technical foul is called then any member of the non-offending team may take the free throw.

Colin Irish, the English international player, poised with the ball to throw to a team-mate.

BASKETBALL

Basketball rules are basically simple but their interpretation, like those of many sports, can be complex. If you look through the rule book, you will appreciate what difficult jobs the referee and umpire have. So, accept their decisions as final and please don't argue with them. Believe me, they really have a thankless task.

To go through the rules in detailed fashion would be unfair to you at this early stage of your basketball development. Therefore the Rules Clinic on the following pages has been designed to help you understand some of the finer points more clearly.

We would like to emphasize that basketball is played by both men and women, and boys and girls. But for simplicity all references are made to he and him. Please don't treat this as any form of chauvinism . . . it's just that it makes it a lot easier!

RULES CLINIC

Can a substitute come on to the court at any time?

He must report to the scorer first and wait for a dead ball situation. Following a violation, only the team who is to inbound the ball is allowed to make a substitution. However, if they do decide to bring a substitute on, then the opposing team are also entitled to do so. It may sound a bit confusing but what it means is that following a violation; the 'guilty' team cannot make a substitution UNLESS the innocent team does.

What is the difference between a violation and a foul?

Both are infringements of the rules but a violation, unlike the foul, is a breach of the rules not involving personal contact. The penalty for a violation is loss of the ball to the opposing team who take a throw-in from the side-line nearest to where the violation took place.

If a basket is scored either during or immediately after a violation has been committed, does the goal stand?

No.

Is there any time limit for a substitute to enter the game?

No, but he must do so as quickly as possible in order to keep the game flowing. If, in the opinion of the official, there is an undue delay then a time-out will be charged against the offending team.

Can a player involved in a jump-ball be substituted?

No.

When does the thirty-seconds clock start?

The moment a team takes possession. It is stopped as soon as possession is lost.

BASKETBALL

If a player takes a three-point throw at the basket and is clearly outside the three-point area at the time of the throw but his momentum, either on the ground or through the air, carries him inside the three-point area, is the basket worth two or three points if successful?

Three. The location of the player is deemed by where his feet are touching the floor. So, even if he leaps through the air to make the throw, he was deemed to be outside the area at the time of the throw because that is where his feet were last positioned on the floor.

If the ball goes out-of-bounds during a team's possession and they have the right to take the throw-in, does a new thirty-seconds period start?

No.

At what point is a player said to be 'in control of the ball'?

When he is holding or dribbling a live ball, or when the ball is at his disposal in an out-of-bounds situation.

What happens at the jump-ball if the ball hits the floor before either player touches the ball?

It is re-taken.

At the jump-ball can players stand where they want around the centre circle?

Yes, but no two players of the same team may occupy adjacent positions if a member of the opposing team wants one of the positions.

What happens if a non-jumper enters the centre circle during the jump-ball?

It is a violation and is penalized accordingly.

Can a player leave the court in order to gain some sort of advantage?

No. A technical foul will be called against the player and two free throws awarded.

Can a goal be scored by the ball entering the basket from underneath?

No. The ball must enter the basket from above it.

OK, so what happens if the ball DOES go through the basket from underneath?

The ball becomes dead and play is re-started with a jump-ball from the nearest circle. However, if it was deliberately thrown through the basket then it is a violation and the opposing team is entitled to a throw-in from the side-line nearest to where the incident took place.

Can a defensive player prevent a shot from entering the basket?

Yes and no. He can attempt to stop a shot provided the ball is on its *upward flight*. However, if it is on its downward flight he cannot interfere with it. The restriction comes to an end once the ball hits the ring, or it is apparent it is going to miss the ring. In case of such a violation the basket will be deemed to have been made and the appropriate points awarded and play re-started from behind the end-line.

Can a player interfere with the ring or backboard to hinder a shot?

Where do you think these up from? Of course not . . . it's not very sportsmanlike is it?

If I'm in possession of the ball and an opponent touches the ball, does the clock re-start for the thirty-seconds rule purpose?

No.

How long does a player have to throw the ball in after a successful free throw or after it has gone out-of-bounds?

Five seconds. Any player taking a free throw must also do so within five seconds of the ball being placed at his disposal.

What happens if, because of so many player fouls, one team is down to only two men?

No problem, play continues with five men playing two. However, if a team is down to only one man the game is stopped and that team loses by forfeit.

If a game is lost by forfeit how is the score recorded?

If the non-offending team is in the lead at the time, then the score stands. If, by some remarkable result, they happened to be trailing, then a score of 2–0 in their favour is recorded.

Can a player shoot and score from anywhere on the court?

Yes. Don't forget, shots from outside the three-point area are worth three points if successful.

Can you go over the difference between personal and technical fouls again?

Certainly . . . contact with an opponent, even if it is during a dead-ball situation or when time is dead, is a personal foul. Fouls that do not involve contact with another player are technical fouls; *i.e.* preventing a shot entering a basket, or unsportsmanlike behaviour.

Can a technical foul therefore be called at a time other than when play is taking place?

Yes. It can be called during the interval or even before the game is started. The penalty is two free throws, after which the game will be re-started in the normal way, *i.e.* with a jump-ball.

If a player shoots for the basket and time is called before the ball enters it, do the points count?

Yes, provided the ball was in flight when time was called. Even if the ball hits the ring, rebounds, and enters the basket, the score still counts.

Does this also apply if the thirty-seconds time-limit expires during a throw?

Yes.

You said a coach can call two time-outs in each half. If he only calls one in the first half can he call three in the second?

No.

When is the ball out-of-bounds?

When it touches a player who is out-of-bounds, or any other person, the floor or any object on or outside a boundary line, or the supports or back of the backboards. A player is said to be out-of-bounds when he touches the floor on or outside the boundary lines.

What is a disqualifying foul?

A foul so bad that the official deems it necessary to dismiss the player from the court forthwith.

If a game goes into overtime, how are ends decided?

By the toss of a coin. At the start of each subsequent period of extra play the teams change ends automatically.

If a foul is committed at the same time as the timekeeper indicates the end of the half or the match, does play continue?

If free throws are part of the punishment, then time must be permitted for them to be taken.

Who takes the throw-in if the ball goes out-of-bounds?

Normally, a member of the team who did NOT last touch the ball. However, if a player deliberately throws the ball at an opponent to cause the ball to go out-of-bounds, then that player's team has possession even though he was the last one to touch the ball before it went out.

RULES · CLINIC

When dribbling, is there any restriction on the number of steps a player may take when he is not in contact with the ball?

No, he may take as many steps as he wants between bounces of a dribble . . . but he won't want to take too many otherwise he would lose possession of the ball.

Who takes the throw-in if two players touch the ball simultaneously before it goes out-of-bounds?

No one. The referee re-starts play with a jump-ball in the nearest circle.

Is play re-started with a jump-ball if the ball lodges on the ring of the basket?

Yes, from the nearest circle.

What is the penalty if a player commits a foul while his team is in possession of the ball?

A foul will be called against him and the opposing team will take possession by taking a throw-in from the side-line nearest to where the foul was committed.

Can a dribbler deliberately run into an opponent in order to get a personal foul against him?

You're certainly a bad sport aren't you? Of course he can't. The dribbler should take what action he can to get past his opponent(s). Until he gets his head and shoulders past the opponent(s) the responsibility to get out of the way rests with the dribbler.

What exactly are the penalties for fouls?

Normal personal foul: The non-offending team has a throw-in from out-of-bounds at the side-line nearest where the foul was committed. This does not apply when the one-plus-one rule is in force (see Game Guide).

Foul on player in act of shooting: If the goal is made then it stands. In addition one free throw is allowed. If the goal is missed then two or three free throws are allowed depending on whether it was originally a two- or three-point attempt at goal.

Intentional and disqualifying fouls: Two free throws are allowed. However, if the foul was against a player in the act of shooting then the penalty is as above. After the free throws (whether successful or not), play is re-started by the team entitled to the free throws taking a throw-in at the mid-court side-line.

What about technical fouls, what are the penalties for them?

As with the personal foul, the offending player will have a foul charged against him and two free throws are awarded to the opposing team. Unlike the personal foul, the free throws can be taken by any player designated by the captain.

Why do players turn to the scorer's table after they have committed a foul and raise their hand?

Because they have to . . . the rules state that they must do this to enable the scorer to identify the guilty party to enable him to register all fouls against him. Remember, five fouls against a player and he is out of the game.

If, after a personal foul, a player other than the fouled player takes the free throw does the successful basket count?

No. And irrespective as to whether it was successful or not the defending team re-starts play with a throw-in from the side-line opposite to the free-throw line.

If two players of opposing sides commit fouls against each other at the same time what happens?

It is called a double foul and the two players involved engage in a jump-ball at the nearest circle.

If two players commit fouls against one player of the opposing side at the same time what is the ruling?

Both players are charged with fouls and two free throws are allowed, unless the player was in the act of shooting when the same penalty as previously mentioned applies.

I know that free throws following a personal foul must be taken by the player fouled. But what happens if he is injured and cannot take the throws?

They must be attempted by his substitute.

Can players not on the court be charged with technical fouls?

Yes. Even the coach and assistant coach can have technical fouls charged against them. Anybody on the team bench so charged will also see two free throws awarded against his team and possession is awarded out-of-bounds at mid-court to the opponents whether they are successful shots or not.

If a team is awarded free throws do they have to take them?

No. At the captain's discretion they may, instead, throw-in from out-of-bounds at the mid-point of the side-line.

RULES · CLINIC

Positions at a free throw
This is where players must stand around the key at a free throw.

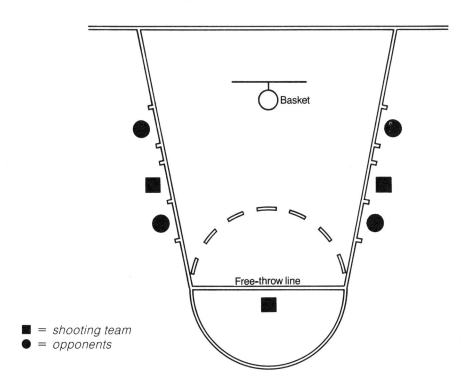

Basket

Free-throw line

■ = *shooting team*
● = *opponents*

When taking free throws who stands where?

Nobody, not even one of the officials, stands inside the free-throw lane. The markers along the edge of the free-throw area indicate where players may stand and the diagram shows clearly who is allowed to occupy each position. Players do not have to occupy those positions, but players of the opposing team must not occupy a position designated for the opposing side.

Right that's about it. We have clearly gone through all aspects of the game, down to some of the finer points of the rules. Now it is time to learn what to do when you get out there on the court.

TECHNIQUE

The first thing you should realize when playing basketball is: **if you haven't got the ball you can't score.** I know that is the case with many sports, but it is never more obvious than in basketball. Possession is very important.

So, how do you get the ball? Apart from free throws after fouls, most possession is gained by a throw-in from the side-line following a violation; from a throw-in after your opponents have scored a basket, or by picking up a loose ball from a wild pass or a rebound.

In the first two instances, your team is handed possession and it is down to you and your team-mates to make sure that possession is retained until an attempt at the basket is made.

You can, of course, also take possession of the ball from an opponent while he is dribbling, or you can intercept a pass.

No matter how you get the ball, remember that basketball is a team passing game. Once you have possession, the ball has to be worked quickly up the court until it reaches one of your players in a good position to score a basket. Often, good attacking moves are spoilt by the shot at the basket being hurried, or taken by a player who was not in as good a position to make the shot as another. So, **vision** is important. Make sure you know where your team-mates are all the time. Believe me, you don't have a great deal of time to plan your next move when you get possession of the ball. That, happily, is one of the reasons why basketball is a success, because it keeps the game fast-moving and fluent.

The team

Basketball is popular because everyone can do everything – there are no positional restrictions. Each member of the team can score and each must defend. However, players are divided into three key types:
(a) the guards
(b) the forwards
(c) the centres.
Let's have a look at the roles of all team members.

The guards Generally the quicker players of a team, they tend to play furthest away from the opposing basket and are the men who initiate attacking moves. Like all players in a team, including the substitutes, the guards will be good handlers of the ball. But they must be specialists at long distance shots or 'driving' to the basket and should be able to pass accurately.

The forwards They normally take up position at the side of the key and should be good shooters from the edge of the key, good passers, normally to the centre, and good rebound players.

The centres Usually the tallest players in the team they are also known as the post, or pivot, players because they take up a position close to the basket, but must be careful not to stay in the restricted area for more than three seconds. Irrespective of their height, they must be good jumpers. Naturally, they must be good close range shooters and rebounders because they are involved in a lot of action around the basket.

TECHNIQUE

2–1–2 attacking formation

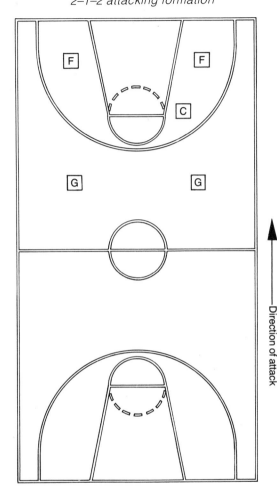

1–2–2 attacking formation

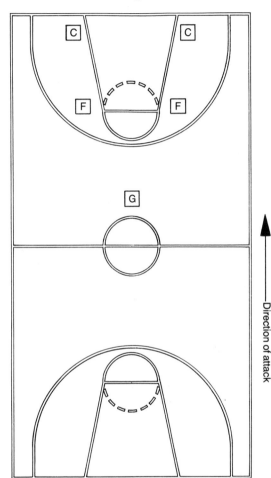

They should also be good passers.

The number of guards, forwards and centres depends upon the state of the match and strength and weakness of the opposition. Most teams will adopt either a 1-2-2 (1 guard, 2 forwards, 2 centres) or 2-1-2 (2 guards, 1 centre, 2 forwards) formation.

Right, that's the players and their roles. But remember that you play both an attacking and defending role while on the court. When your team has possession you are on the attack. Otherwise you have to be a defender, and thus attempt to get possession of the ball, or prevent your opponents scoring. Defence is just as an exciting part of basketball as attack but we will first look at techniques for successful attacking.

The basic skills that all basketball players should master are:
(a) Passing

Passing

Hold the ball close to your body before passing, and spread your fingers around the ball.

(b) Catching
(c) Dribbling
(d) Shooting
(e) Rebound play
   Let us look at each of these skills individually.

PASSING

The golden rule with passing is safety – don't give the ball away. Make sure the ball goes to a player in a more advantageous position than yourself and don't keep the ball in the air too long thus enabling an opponent to intercept it.

The long pass the length of the court (often called the Javelin or Baseball pass) is impressive if it is successful, but the majority of passes should be short-range to a team-mate who, like yourself, is progressing up the court. If you can keep passes down to 3–4.5m (10–15ft) or so, there is less chance of you losing possession. However, don't think that the long-pass is outlawed, it certainly isn't and there are times when it should be used. For example, if a team-mate is standing unguarded near the basket then, by all means, attempt the long pass. But don't get too ambitious to begin with. Make sure you have the feel for conventional short passes before you embark on such adventurous stuff.

The pass should be made with two hands and the ball should be protected before its release, thus giving the opposition less chance of getting it.

Two things to remember about passing are: (1) it is the safest way of keeping possession and, (2) it is a quicker way of getting the ball down the court than

dribbling. So, if you are given the alternatives, pass or dribble, you know which one to choose . . . the pass. Basketball is a **team passing game**.

Some important do's and don'ts of passing:
(a) Make sure the pass is accurate.
(b) Make the pass direct. This prevents an opponent intercepting, or stealing the ball.
(c) Don't pass the ball high in the air. Again, the higher the ball is in the air the longer it is out of your team's possession and thus there is more chance of the steal.
(d) Make sure the pass is well-timed, particularly if the man you are passing to is on the move.

Although there are no restrictions on how the ball is passed (as long as it gets there!), there are three 'named' types of pass:
(a) the chest pass, (b) the overhead pass and (c) the bounce pass.

The chest pass is made with the ball thrown from a chest-high position. It is used more often than any other pass and is employed when there is no defender between you and the player you are passing to.

The ball is held with both hands, and by the fingers and not the palm of the hand. As the pass is executed the whole body moves forward **into** the pass.

The receiver should indicate where he wants the pass sending to by extending his hand. It will invariably be the hand furthest away from the defender, and it is to that arm that the pass should be directed.

The overhead pass is similar to the chest pass but is used to throw the ball over an opponent standing between you and your intended team-mate. It is held with both hands like the chest pass and the target area should again be your team-mate's signalled hand. Keep the ball **in front of your head**, unlike a soccer throw-in, and use your wrists and forearms for power.

The bounce pass is another way of passing with an opponent in the way. This time, instead of passing the ball over him, it is passed 'under' him. The ball is 'passed' to the floor, and a single bounce takes it into your team-mate's hands. The pass should be made from the side of the body (level with the hip) as opposed to starting from a chest position, and is normally made with one hand, as opposed to two. There is a danger that this pass will be intercepted unless it is passed with speed and to a player not too far away from you.

The key points to remember about passing are:

(a) Know where the man is you intend passing to.
(b) Keep your eyes on the target you are aiming at.
(c) Aim at your team-mate's hand which is furthest away from his defender.
(d) Follow-through with your arms after executing the pass.

Once you have made the pass don't think that's the end of your role. It most certainly isn't. You should always be moving around the court and ready to take either the return pass or another pass later in the play.

BASKETBALL

The chest pass

The start position.

When executing the pass, move 'into' the throw and don't stand still.

The follow through. Note how the fingers are pointing in the direction of the throw.

TECHNIQUE

The overhead pass

The start position.

Hold the ball directly above your head and fix your eyes on the target.

Step forward into the throw as it is made but keep the ball in front of your head, unlike the soccer throw.

Snap your wrists to make the throw.

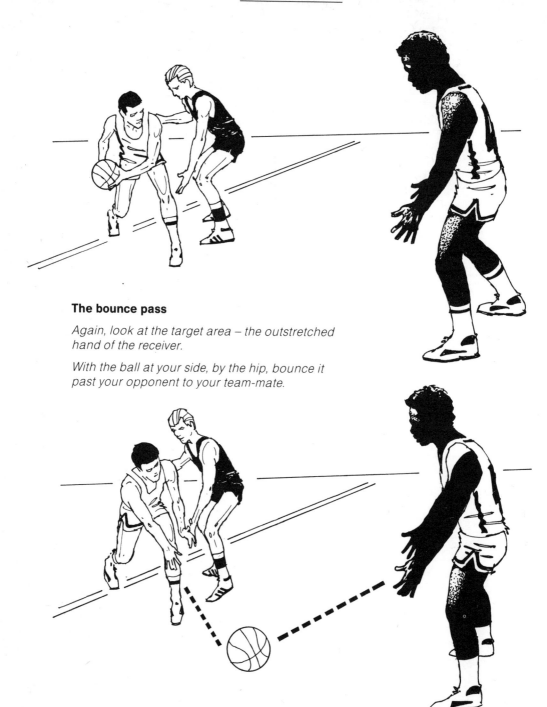

The bounce pass

Again, look at the target area – the outstretched hand of the receiver.

With the ball at your side, by the hip, bounce it past your opponent to your team-mate.

Passing

Make the pass to the receiver's 'target area'. In this case, it is his outstretched right hand.

CATCHING

There is nothing more infuriating than losing possession because a team-mate has not been able to hold a good pass. So, take note of the following points and you will ALWAYS be able to catch a ball without giving it away:

The first thing to remember at all times is **keep your eye on the ball**. This cannot be emphasized too strongly. If you are always watching the ball it will reduce the risk of error.

You must always give the passer a target to aim at and you should indicate with your hand where you want the ball passing to. Once the pass has been made to you, take the ball with two hands and with your fingers well spread around the ball. Keep your eyes on the ball until it is safely in your possession. Once you have got the ball don't stand there nursing it. Get it safely under control ready for either a pass, shot or dribble. The quicker you can control the ball the quicker you can effect your next move. Don't forget, basketball is a fast game. Don't rush, but if you slow it down too much then you may throw away any advantage your team has.

When catching the ball don't bounce it once and re-catch it because this prevents you from then dribbling; you are deemed to have dribbled by doing that. So don't get into that bad habit from the start. Once you have caught the ball, quickly decide what you are going to do; pass again, shoot or dribble.

Jeff Jones, protecting the ball from a defender and looking for a team-mate to pass to.

BASKETBALL

Dribbling

Dribbling is done with the fingers and pads of the hand, not the palm. Don't 'slap' the ball.

If you dribble with the ball too far in front of you, you are inviting a 'steal' from the opposition.

DRIBBLING

Passing is the most effective way of moving the ball around the court. Now for another way; dribbling.

A good dribbler is a hard man to dispossess and, as we said earlier, if you don't have possession of the ball you can't score any points. So being able to dribble is a skill that every player should develop.

Dribbling is made with the fingers and pad of the hand, not the palm. The ball should not be 'slapped' but pushed down firmly, with the wrist playing a big part of the action.

As a novice you should practice dribbling by initially standing still, and then gradually moving around. Don't bounce the ball too far in front of you because, if you were in a match, your opponent would have an easy job dispossessing you.

After you have practised for a while you should have got the feel of the ball and the bounce. The next stage is to practise bouncing without looking at the ball. Top players dribble while looking to see where their team-mates and opponents are at all times.

Make sure only one hand comes into contact with the ball. If both touch the ball then the dribble is deemed to be over. You have been warned.

Keep the ball between knee and waist height while dribbling and vary your dribbling between hands. It is no good being able to dribble with the right hand only. Your opponents will soon exploit this weakness. You must be able to dribble with both hands. You must also be able to vary your pace when dribbling so you can take an opponent unaware and go past him at speed.

Remember, basketball is a team-game, and while dribbling keeps you in possession of the ball it is doing the team no good if there is someone better placed to score. So, keep your eyes on the game, not the ball, and as soon as you see a team-mate in an ideal or better position than you pass to him immediately.

SHOOTING

It is not right to say shooting is the most important element of basketball, because all skills are equally important. But let's be honest, if you cannot shoot then you aren't going to get any points and, after all, that's what the game is about.

Any player can shoot from anywhere on the court where there are no restrictions. But common sense will tell you that the closer you are to the basket the more chance there is of success. However, there will be occasions, when your team is trailing, and long distance shots (from outside the three-point circle) should be attempted in order to reduce the deficit in points.

TECHNIQUE

Opposite *A good dribbler has no need to look at the ball, his eyes should be looking around the court for the next move.*

Ideally, the ball should be kept between knee and waist height when dribbling.

BASKETBALL

The lay-up

The lay-up is one of the most frequently used ways of scoring.

There are five basic types of shot:
(a) Lay-up shots
(b) Set shots
(c) Jump shots
(d) Free-throw shots
(e) Close-up shots

The lay-up shot

Used when an attacker gets the ball and, seeing no defender between him and the basket, dribbles in to the basket and jumps to shoot the ball off the backboard and into the basket. The lay-up shot will invariably be made from the right- or left-hand side of the basket. If it is made to the right, the shot is made with the right hand, and take-off is from the left foot. The sequence is, of course, the other way round if the shot is to the left side of the basket. Don't forget though, after getting hold of the ball with both hands while dribbling, you are entitled only to two more steps so, step two should be your take-off step.

When releasing the ball, take advantage of the backboard. You don't have to throw the ball directly into the basket. If you play it gently to the square on the backboard above the ring, the ball will drop into the basket. If you hit the square too hard then the ball will most likely rebound away from the basket.

The set shot

The set shot is used when, unlike the lay-up, there is an opponent between you and the basket, but far enough away not to impede you.

With the set shot, stance is important. Your feet should point in the direction of the shot and your shoulders should be facing squarely to the basket. While the ball is held with both hands the shot is actually only made with one hand – the shooting hand. The ball rests on the finger pads of that hand. The non-shooting hand supports the ball at the side.

The ball should be released from slightly above the head. Your eyes should be fixed firmly on the target, which can be either the ring itself or the target on the backboard. Either way, build up a mental picture of the shot.

Your legs should be slightly bent when adopting your stance and straightened as the throw is made. This gives you more power. Don't forget the snap of the wrist as you make the throw. This helps to impart backspin on the ball. And don't forget the follow-through.

The set shot

The stance.

Bring the ball up in front of your face.

Straighten your legs as the ball is delivered.

Concentrate on the target.

Follow through and flick your wrist.

The jump shot

The jump shot is played in the same way as the set shot except the ball is delivered while jumping. It is used when a defender is in the way and you make space by jumping, thus giving the defender less opportunity to block the shot.

The jump is made horizontally and the ball is delivered at the top of the jump just like the set shot. However, the inexperienced player will find this shot a difficult one to master initially. So don't attempt it until you've learned to master the set shot.

The jump shot

Preparation. Fix your eyes on the target and keep your knees slightly bent.

Bend your knees more, bringing the ball to head height.

TECHNIQUE

Jump off the ground and deliver the shot at the top of the jump. Make sure the jump is straight up – don't jump forward.

Follow through and flick your wrists.

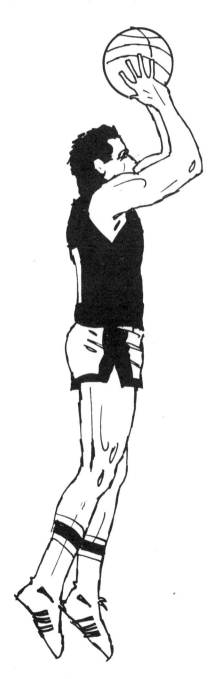

The free-throw shot

This is more or less the same as the set shot. It is awarded after a foul and every player in a team will at some stage during a match have to make a free throw. It is therefore important that you are a good free thrower.

It is like a penalty kick in soccer and the battle is between you and the basket. No other player can get in your way to prevent you scoring.

You must stand with your feet behind the free-throw line. The technique thereafter is the same as the set throw.

The beauty of the free throw is that you can practise it as much as you like and when you come to a match situation you will be faced with an identical throw. There is, of course, a matter of nerves to overcome in a match which, funnily, don't appear when you are practising on your own. Nevertheless, you must practise the free throw shot. There is no excuse for missing it.

The free throw

Keep your eyes on the basket and knees bent.

Start to straighten your legs and shooting arm.

Flick your wrist and follow through. The ball is on its way to another successful basket . . . we hope.

Clyde Vaughan, the English international player, showing off his phenomenal shooting ability.

The dunk – *the player jumps into the air and throws the ball down through the basket.*

Close-in shots

There are occasions when you will be close to the basket and none of the previously mentioned throws can be practically carried out. This is when improvization comes in and one of the most effective close-in shots is the *dunk*. Simply it is a shot by a player who jumps high and throws (or dunks) the ball down into the basket. But this is an extremely difficult shot because the basket is 3m (10ft) off the ground.

Another close-in shot is the **hook**, which is a 'mini' version of the lay-up. It will quite often be carried out by a shooter getting the ball while he has his back to the basket. He then pivots, steps and jumps to make the shot. Unlike the dunk it is not a powerful shot but a gentle one and the wrist imparts a lot of back spin as the ball hits the ring or backboard.

The hook shot

Getting ready for the hook. Note the position of the fingers and, of course, how the eyes are fixed on the target.

Keep the throwing arm outstretched, even after the ball has gone. The fingers impart a great deal of backspin on the ball.

REBOUND · PLAY

A great percentage of shots are rebounded off the backboard or the ring. This is where players under the basket must be aware of what is happening because the ball is going begging and there is a 50-50 chance of your team getting possession.

Being alert, and able to anticipate the shot and rebound are the key to good rebounding play. Good team-work and knowledge of your team-mates' skills is also a help. For example, you need to know which players are regular three-point shooters.

The centre and the forwards are generally the players assigned to rebounding duties and they should, when they anticipate a shot from a colleague, get into position in the key in readiness for a rebound. They must, bearing in mind a defender will also be in

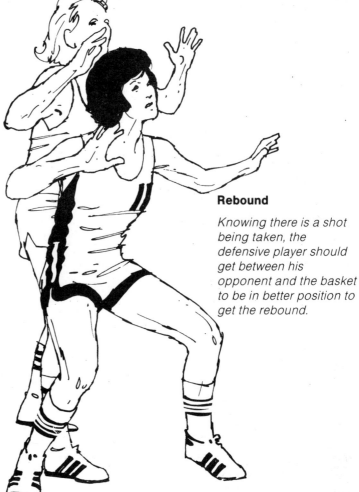

Rebound

Knowing there is a shot being taken, the defensive player should get between his opponent and the basket to be in better position to get the rebound.

there trying to do the same thing, get into the most advantageous position before their opponent.

The rebound shot is totally unpredictable and again improvization is necessary. If possible, the ball should be collected with both hands from the rebound, and a shot made on the jump. But often it will be a case of jumping and quickly tipping the ball into the net.

So that's it from the attacker's point of view. It all sounded easy didn't it? Now we'll make the game a bit harder because we are going to introduce the defenders and look at their role and how they try to prevent the attackers from passing, catching, dribbling, shooting, and winning rebounds.

DEFENSIVE · PLAY

The best defence is one which makes life as tough as possible for the attacking side. Harass your opponent as much as you can, without making contact with him and be prepared to help when a team-mate is beaten. There is no point in just stopping your man from scoring – it's a team game!

When standing in front of an attacker it is not only the body that should be used as a form of defence. Effective use must be made of the arms, without making contact with your opponent of course. If the attacker

Defending against the shooter

Timing is the all-important thing to remember when defending a shot.

BASKETBALL

attempts a shot you should have your arms in the air to challenge him. The palms of the hands should be facing the ball and ready to take possession of it if the chance arises.

You should always have your knees bent ready to make a move or jump if necessary and know where the ball and the player you are marking are.

Anticipation is the key to successful defence. That way you will prevent an attacker making a drive for the net because once he is past you there is nothing you can do about it.

TECHNIQUE

Don't be taken in – you could get sold a dummy!

Your opponent prepares to shoot . . . you jump to defend and what happens next? He changes his mind.

BASKETBALL

Joel Moore, England's most outstanding guard.

Defending against the ball handler

Keep your arms up in the air if your opponent is attempting a pass, or if dribbling, keep one hand low by the ball without contacting the player.

Always make life tough for the player receiving a pass.

TECHNIQUE

You must always make it difficult for your opponent to pass and shoot. Likewise, you should be alert and try and outwit your opponent at any rebound.

A good defender is one who knows the strengths and weaknesses of his opponents. If the man you are marking is, for example, only good at dribbling with his right hand, then you defend that side of him thus restricting his movement with the ball.

Because basketball is a no-contact sport the onus, more often than not, is on the defender to make sure contact is not made. You must be aware of this at all times, and be very careful. But a good defender will not need to make contact. He will be able to read the game well enough to make life tough for the attacking team.

Remember, defending is not just about gaining possession or forcing an error. It is about forcing the opponents out of their time limit as well. They have ten seconds to get the ball out of their own half, and thirty seconds in which to take a shot. Good defending can force them to forfeit the ball on either of those grounds. Quite often you will see an entire team employ a **full court press** which is a defensive tactic designed at keeping the opponents in their own half for the requisite 10 seconds. It is very effective when it comes off.

Important defensive points to remember are:
(1) Always position yourself between the man and the basket, but deny him the ball.
(2) Always make sure you get back to your basket before the attacking team does.

That's about it, except a final mention about practice. The beauty of basketball is that three of the game's fundamentals, passing, dribbling and shooting, can be practiced on your own. (Use a wall to throw different passes against.)

In all sports it is essential to practise, and practise regularly. More important you should enjoy practising, but I'm sure you will enjoy basketball practice, whether it be on your own or with team-mates.

Basketball is a great game to play and watch. We hope that through *Play the Game* you have become more aware of the finer points of the sport no matter whether you are a player or spectator. If you are a player then we have done our bit, and the rest is up to you . . . go out and play the game, and enjoy it.

USEFUL ADDRESSES

English Basket Ball Association (EBBA)
Calomax House
Lupton Avenue
Leeds
LS9 7EE
Tel: (0532) 496044

International Basketball Federation (FIBA)
Rugendasse Strasse 19
Munich
West Germany

National Basketball Association (NBA)
Olympic Tower
645 5th Avenue
New York
NY 10022
USA

Amateur Basketball Association (ABA)
1750 East Boulder Street
Colorado Springs
Colorado 80909
USA

**Here T J Robinson (No. 11) blocks Nic
Burns, the 7ft tall English international.**

RULES CLINIC

INDEX

Butch Hayes shows his prowess at the dunk. He is 6ft 1in tall, the basket is 10ft from the ground.

INDEX